Spies, Soldiers, Couriers, and Saboteurs: Women of the American Revolution

K.M. Waldvogel

Claire and Evelyn,
*   Hope you enjoy!*

*   K. M. Waldvogel*

Orange Hat Publishing
www.orangehatpublishing.com - Waukesha, WI

Spies, Soldiers, Couriers, and Saboteurs:
Women of the American Revolution
Copyrighted © 2019 K.M. Waldvogel
ISBN 978-1-64538-047-4
Library of Congress Control Number: 2019905806
First Edition

Spies, Soldiers, Couriers, and Saboteurs:
Women of the American Revolution
by K.M. Waldvogel

For information, please contact:

Orange Hat Publishing
www.orangehatpublishing.com
Waukesha, WI

www.orangehatpublishing.com

This book is dedicated to all the women—known and unknown—who helped our country gain its independence. They saw a need and stepped forward, risking their freedom and their lives for a country they loved. May their patriotism and selfless acts inspire generations to come.

Acknowledgements

I believe that every writer appreciates support and encouragement while struggling through the writing process. That is one of the many reasons I am so grateful for my husband and family. Their love and strength buoyed me whenever I felt I was in over my head.

I'm also thankful to my many friends who graciously read my writing and prompted me to finish this project, especially Mary Rangel, my childhood friend and greatest fan.

Thank you to the Yarnspinners (a Wisconsin Writers Association critique group) and the Scottsdale Writing Critique Group for your suggestions, insight, and helpful comments offered to improve my work. You taught me the importance of careful revisions and edits and reminded me that tomorrow is another opportunity to write even more!

I feel blessed to have all of you in my life.

Author Note

Research is like traveling. Often hidden gems of peaceful lakes or beautiful mountains reveal themselves when "side trips" are taken on a journey. Similarly, I discovered stories of many courageous women when I began my research journey. One story led to another.

I delved into the subject and devoured nonfiction books and magazine articles about these women. I scoured the Internet for websites that displayed primary sources confirming facts I had uncovered. I corresponded with historical societies and visited historical museums seeking accurate information. And I had the honor of speaking with one woman's descendant, who provided details of her heroic actions.

While I strived to be as accurate as possible concerning these women and the circumstances of their decisions, I also found some information difficult to confirm. This was not surprising to me since these women lived several hundred years ago. However, I did my best.

When writing dialog or describing each woman's feelings, I attempted to put myself in her place and imagine the stress and fear she endured. With each story, I grew more in awe of the bravery displayed by these women.

I am thrilled to tell their stories.

TABLE OF CONTENTS

INTRODUCTION

In the mid-1700s, tensions mounted between the American colonies and Britain. Eventually war broke out. Many men answered the call to arms. And so did many women. Not content to be bystanders, women took active roles in the conflict by spying, carrying messages, fighting, and sabotaging the enemy.

But what caused the tensions? Why would people who had lived under Britain's rule and protection decide to turn their backs on this powerful country and form a new nation?

In order to understand this, it is important to look at events leading to this decision. At that time, many European countries competed with one another to own land in America. They fought to gain control because of the riches offered by the New World. In particular, France and Britain were each determined to claim the land as their own. This resulted in the French and Indian War. This first worldwide war, fought from Asia to the Americas, ended with Britain eventually winning.

The cost of this was steep. Britain had borrowed heavily to finance the war and faced the repayment of those debts. Parts of those costs had been spent defending the colonies in North America. Because the British Parliament felt the colonists should bear the burden for the expenses, it enacted tax laws to which many Americans objected.

In 1764, England passed the Sugar Act, which taxed many goods coming into America. While the Sugar Act reduced the tax on imported molasses, it added a duty on many other goods previously not taxed, such as sugar, some wines, printed calico cloth, and coffee. This cost the merchants money and hurt the economy in the New World.

A year later, Parliament enacted the Stamp Act, requiring that all "printed paper" must include a "stamp" showing a tax had been paid. It taxed newspapers, other publications, legal documents, playing cards, and other materials. This act, which affected everyone not only merchants, was especially unpopular. Colonists viewed this as unfair. Although they had to pay these taxes, they felt they did not have their opinions represented in Parliament. So the slogan, "No taxation without representation," became popular.

To make matters worse, Parliament passed the Quartering Act requiring colonists to give room and board to British soldiers and forage for their horses. Depending on the needs or whims of the officers, families could be ordered out of their homes completely. At other times, soldiers resided in the houses while family members were confined to specific rooms. Many colonists resented this, feeling this was a violation of their rights. Housing soldiers in private homes saved the British Army money. So despite the objections, this practice continued.

The passage of these laws created a division among the colonists. Some people, called Tories or Loyalists, agreed with the British Government. They felt Americans should abide by these rules and remain loyal to Britain. Others felt that the colonists should break away and govern themselves. These people, called Whigs or Patriots, rebelled and fought against the British in any way they could.

Since these laws negatively affected family finances and businesses, many women supported the rebellion. They dreamed of independence and a world without interference from Britain. Their involvement in the revolution took many different forms, but all of these women risked their lives.

Molly Rinker spied on the British and secretly sent information to the Patriots. Grace and Rachel Martin intercepted an enemy dispatch and delivered it to a general of the Continental Army. Anna Maria Lane disguised herself and fought in battles. These women, and others, helped the Patriots during the American Revolution but receive only a footnote in history lessons.

While their stories all differ, each woman stood up for what she believed. The burning desire to aid her new country's independence drove each one to risk her life for the Patriots' cause. Their roles were often unheralded and undiscovered, but these women's contributions were invaluable. They were true American patriots. This book tells the stories of a few.

CHAPTER ONE

The Female Highwaymen

South Carolina, 1780

Peeking out from behind a thicket of trees, sisters-in-law Grace and Rachel Martin, disguised as men, waited for the British courier and his guards. Nothing stirred. Silence except for the occasional hoot from an owl or squirrels scurrying through leaves. *Why didn't they come? Was the information correct? Would they pass this way?* Waiting, waiting, waiting.

Silence mounted. Grace Martin, the younger woman, let her mind wander as she recalled the events of the last few days. Rumors had circulated that a British courier would pass through the area tonight. He carried information for high-ranking officers, but what was in those papers? Did the intelligence affect her husband—and Rachel's—who both served under Nathanael Greene, Commander of the Continental Army in the South? The possibility of peril to their husbands ripped at her heart. The dispatch needed to be intercepted. But how? Who could help?

"That messenger's not getting through," Grace had fumed to Rachel. "Somebody needs to stop him. Think! Who can we trust?"

She'd continued ranting as she paced the back room of their mother-in-law's house. "Who knows what's in that dispatch? We need to get that information to General Greene."

The women had eliminated one possibility after another. Many of the able-bodied men had left to join the militia. The few who remained were scattered across the countryside. How could the women find volunteers?

Finally, Rachel turned to her sister-in-law. "If you were courageous," she'd taunted, "I'd ask you to help me with a plan to rob that courier."

Grace had bristled. "I'm as courageous as any!"

"In that case," Rachel said, pleased that Grace took the bait, "here's what we do—if you're up to it."

Grace listened and smiled. Perfect. The two women would dress as highwaymen and steal the dispatch. With night's darkness shielding them, they couldn't be identified. Who would suspect them?

The women had rummaged through their husbands' old clothing for disguises. They donned britches and old shirts. They shoved their hair under wide-brimmed hats. Satisfied with their appearance, the two conspirators raced to intercept the messenger.

Now they waited for the unsuspecting travelers. Finally, the clomp of hooves announced approaching riders. It seemed like hours while the women waited for the men to round the curve in the road. Grace and Rachel adjusted their hats, lowered their heads, and leapt in front of the enemy while brandishing their weapons.

Startled at the sight of the duo, the British courier and guards reined in their horses. They exchanged puzzled looks, guards reaching for their weapons. The women leveled their pistols at the men causing them to freeze.

"Hands off your weapons. Turn over your dispatch," Grace demanded in a gruff voice. "Now!"

The courier glanced at the soldiers who'd been caught unprepared. He returned his gaze toward Rachel who cocked her pistol. Resigned to the outcome, he fumbled for his dispatch and retrieved it. While Rachel took it, Grace withdrew documents from her pocket.

"This is a parole," Grace stated as she shoved papers in front of the men. "It states that you will not fight against the Americans and you will not encourage anyone to fight against them. Each of you sign here and you can go free. If not…" Grace's voice trailed in a threatening manner.

After a slight hesitation, the men signed the document, turned their horses, and galloped back in the direction from which they came. Meanwhile, Grace and Rachel scrambled through the woods. They fought through the brush and brambles to reach their destination, the home of a trusted Whig.

Panting, they pounded on the door until the older man answered.

"Take this to General Greene," Grace insisted thrusting the papers at him. "Right away. Hurry!"

"What? What is it?" he asked, puzzled at the demand.

"A British dispatch," Rachel explained. "We just took it from a messenger. It needs to get to General Greene. Please."

The man stared at Grace and Rachel in amazement, but recognized the urgency. Grabbing his coat and hat, he mounted his horse and rode off clasping the dispatch close to him.

Wishing him luck, the women stole through the night, taking a shortcut to the property of their mother-in-law, Elizabeth Martin, where they lived. Once home, the two women removed their husbands' clothing, donned their own, and shook out their hair. They smiled at one another, pleased with their night's rendezvous. They did it!

Their celebration, though, was short lived as approaching horses announced the arrival of visitors. A knock on the door alarmed the duo. *Had they been recognized? Had someone seen them return to the Martin property?*

Elizabeth opened the door. The British courier and guards stood before her. Grace and Rachel traded nervous glances, their pulses racing. The two women seemed to read one another's mind. *Why had they come? Did the men know of the women's involvement? Had they endangered Elizabeth?* Grace and Rachel moved closer to one another for support.

"Ma'am," the courier began, "we're sorry to disturb you but we hoped you'd provide lodging for us for the night."

"I'm sure I saw you pass earlier," Mrs. Martin stated. "What brings you back?"

Flushing, the man responded, "We were accosted on

the road. Two rebel lads held us at gunpoint. They stole the dispatch I carried and forced us to sign a parole."

"Weren't you armed?" Rachel asked, stepping forward. "Surely you could have shot them."

"They took us by surprise," one of the guards admitted. "We didn't have time to react. They were on us before we knew what was happening."

"How frightening!" Grace remarked, hiding her pleasure. "I can't imagine the nerve of those rebels! Attacking you like that. Well, at least you're safe now."

"Yes, ma'am," the messenger said. "Again, if we could just spend the night…"

"Certainly," Elizabeth replied graciously. "You're welcome to stay here. Rachel, Grace, let's get these gentlemen something to eat."

"Thank you," the courier replied. "We'll leave at first light. We won't be a bother."

The men entered the home, ate the prepared food, and stayed the night. They left the next morning not realizing that their two young hostesses were the "rebel lads" who had accosted them on the road. Grace and Rachel breathed sighs of relief, their secret intact.

* * * * *

While it's uncertain if Elizabeth knew about the actions of her daughters-in-law, undoubtedly she would have approved. She and her husband, Abram, had seven sons and two daughters. The entire family supported the fight for independence and Elizabeth strongly encouraged all her sons to fight for the Patriots. Each of them joined the Continental Army. Several were wounded and one lost his life in the war—William, Grace's husband.

William had been an artillery officer and survived the Sieges of Savannah and Charleston but was killed while tending a cannon at the Siege of Augusta in 1780. Grace, who had married William when she was only fourteen years old, chose not to remarry. Instead, she raised their three young children on her own. She died in 1800.

Barclay Martin, Rachel's husband, returned to his wife after the war. The couple continued to live in South Carolina until Barclay's death in 1815. Several years later, Rachel moved to Tennessee where she died in 1849 at the age of 86.

CHAPTER TWO

Muster at the Ludingtons'

New York, 1777

Sixteen-year-old Sybil Ludington raced through the countryside of New York on her trusted horse, Star, on the night of April 26, 1777. Her task—to awaken members of the militia and call them to arms. With rain striking her face, she pushed onward, determined to make her father proud.

"Awake!" she shouted as she rode through the stormy night alerting the neighbors. "Muster at the Ludingtons!"

Her journey itself was dangerous, and the rain created muddy conditions, hampering her travel. She knew the terrain, though, and plowed forward. With the future of a new country at stake, she rode like the wind to collect volunteers. She could not fail. Her mission too important.

Sybil's father, Henry Ludington, was a colonel in the American militia. Earlier that night a messenger braved the storm, arriving at the Ludington household.

"Colonel Ludington!" he had called, pounding on the door. "Colonel, I have news."

Ludington answered and pulled the rain-soaked man inside.

"Colonel, the British are marching to Danbury! They'll be there shortly." The messenger, breathing hard, collapsed onto a chair. "I realized the danger. As soon as I heard, I rode here. It wasn't an easy journey."

The man relayed his experience between gasps. He had ridden the 25 miles from Danbury, his horse sloshing over rain-soaked roads. As he told his tale, Sybil watched her father's brow furrow in concern until finally he interrupted the messenger.

"They'll find our supplies, our munitions," Ludington said. "We have to stop them. If we don't, it's over."

"Yes sir, but how?"

"It's planting time. The men are at their farms. Muster

everyone possible. Go now. Scour the countryside. Tell the men to meet here."

"Sir, I can't," the man had insisted. "I'm exhausted. I rode for hours to get here. I can't go on. My horse can't go on."

"You have to. If we don't stop the British, we're doomed."

"I barely made it here. I can't. Maybe a neighbor, someone close by."

Sybil realized her father's dilemma. She knew he needed someone familiar with the area to warn the militia quickly so he could organize the best defense. They were scattered throughout the countryside. How could he gather them? If they didn't move right away, all was lost.

"I can go," Sybil volunteered.

"No!" her mother protested. "It's too dangerous. You're too young."

Stepping in front of her mother, Sybil looked into her father's eyes. She spoke with confidence.

"Father, I know the area. You need the men as soon as possible. You can't wait. I promise you I can do this."

Hesitating momentarily, her father relented. "I will allow it. This is the route I want you to follow," he said drawing a crude map for her.

Despite her mother's concerns, Sybil mounted Star and

headed into the night, thunder and lightning crackling overhead. She knew the stakes.

As she urged Star through the countryside, she was aware of many possible dangers ahead. This was hostile country with Indians, wild animals, "cowboys" who were on the side of the British, and "skinners" who had no ties to the British or Americans but simply robbed and murdered their victims.

Pushing her concerns aside, Sybil flew through the night. The stakes were too high to hesitate. Her father—and her country—depended on her. She would not let them down.

She followed the circuitous route her father had planned for her, past homes of militia volunteers. Time and again she called out, "The British are in Danbury. Hurry, muster at the Ludingtons."

After her forty-mile ride, Sybil was exhausted. Star lathered. Rain unrelenting. She had never ridden so hard in her life. However, the young woman returned to her home the next morning to discover nearly 400 volunteers gathered at the Ludington home, ready to defend their land and freedom. There was hope!

The men marched to town to confront the enemy. They arrived too late to stop the British from destroying most supplies and burning much of Danbury. However, the militia confronted the enemy's troops, forced them back to their ships in the Long Island Sound, obstructing their advance. Sybil's courageous efforts helped make this possible.

Her ride that night was not the first time she showed courage and stepped forward to help her father. He and his men often sabotaged the British attempts to obtain munitions or supplies. As a result, the British offered a large reward for Ludington's head. Hoping to capture him and claim the reward, a Loyalist, Ichobod Prosser, planned to raid the Ludingtons' home.

"We can surround the house and make sure he won't escape," Prosser had said. "We'll get that reward."

He expected to sneak into the house and kidnap the colonel without incident. Prosser didn't realize the colonel was out with the militia and wasn't home that night. Ludington's wife and children, though, occupied the house and kept guard.

Sybil and her sister, Rebecca, saw the men approaching. Their father had taught the girls how to watch over the house and keep it safe. They alerted the rest of the household.

"Mary, get up, quick. Put candles in all the windows," Sybil instructed. "Mother, help with the candles and then stay out of sight with the little ones. Archibald, Derick, take these rifles. March back and forth in front of the windows like soldiers. Rebecca and I will march on the porch."

With the help of their younger brothers and sisters, Sybil and Rebecca tricked the men. Prosser believed the house too heavily defended and too risky to continue. They dropped their plan and fled. The Ludingtons had fooled the enemy.

Courage, loyalty, and hard work continued to be a part of Sybil's life. At the age of 23, she married a farmer, Edmond Ogden, and they eventually had a son, Henry. When her husband died from yellow fever in 1799, Sybil needed to provide for herself and her son. She applied for and received a license as an innkeeper, an unusual job for a woman during that time. Through determination and perseverance, Sybil continued to take care of herself and Henry, who eventually became a lawyer.

Later she moved to Unadilla, New York, along with Henry and his wife. Sybil passed away in 1839 at the age of 78. This patriotic woman was buried in the Maple Avenue Cemetery in Patterson, New York, where her father was also buried.

* * * * *

Sybil lived an unassuming life, receiving little recognition for her patriotic efforts. She didn't seek attention but preferred to tend to her everyday duties and obligations. This seems fitting for a woman who saw a need and simply stepped up to do it.

Now, hundreds of years later, history has recognized and honored her. In 1961, a statue showing Sybil on her horse, Star, was built in Carmel, New York, and the route she rode in 1777 is marked by signs along the roadside in Putnam County. Also as a tribute to her, the U.S. Postal Service issued a stamp in her honor in 1975. Her ride that fateful night displayed true heroism.

CHAPTER THREE

A Hard Secret to Swallow

South Carolina, 1781

"Halt! Where are you headed?"

A British scout stepped into the middle of the road, musket in hand.

Eighteen-year-old Emily Geiger reined in her horse and stammered, "I...I am on my w-way to my uncle's house."

"Rebels are in the area. What do you know about them?" The scout stared at the young girl. His dark eyes pierced through her.

Emily's cheeks burned under his scrutiny and her voice failed. She tried to meet his eyes, but his uniform—red long coat, white breeches, and black boots—screamed authority. He glared at her. Her heart pounding, she avoided his gaze. She could not lie without shaking inside.

"Dismount and come with me!" the scout commanded.

The young woman obeyed and followed him to Fort Granby, South Carolina, about a mile away. Once inside, the scout brought her before the commanding officer, a tall, fit man with a no-nonsense attitude.

"Why are you on this road?" Lord Francis Rawdon snapped, eying the girl with disheveled hair and rumpled clothing.

"I...I am going to visit my uncle."

"And the purpose of the visit?"

"Um...I...he is my uncle. I travel to see him every few months."

"And his name?"

"Uncle Jacob. Jacob Geiger."

"Is anyone traveling with you?"

She shook her head.

"A young woman alone? Out here?" Rawdon continued. His brow furrowed.

"I...I have traveled it before. I know the way."

"On your travels, did you come across any rebels?"

"Rebels? Umm…no…I…no, I saw no one."

The officer studied her for a moment. The moment felt like hours to Emily.

"Come with me," he directed and led her to a small room. Turning to a soldier, he barked, "Have a matron search her." With that, he slammed the door.

Alone, Emily wondered what to do. General Nathanael Greene of the Continental Army was depending on her. How would she get out of this mess?

She thought back to the events of the past several days. General Greene's camp was close to her family's home. The general had struck up a friendship with her father and had become a frequent visitor to their home. On one of his visits, she had overheard him tell her father that Rawdon was abandoning the fort, believing it too far from reinforcements. The British planned to return to Charleston.

"This could be our chance," Greene had explained. "Rawdon will be out in the open and if I can get reinforcements from General Sumter, we will have Rawdon outnumbered. I know we can defeat him. I just need to get word to Sumter. But my men are weak, malnourished. This would mean riding seventy miles or more. I don't know…"

Emily's crippled father listened intently. "Maybe a civilian volunteer. I would go if I could."

"I thought of that, but no luck so far. I cannot say I blame them. The area is thick with Tories. If a messenger were caught, he would be arrested for sure."

"There must be someone. Let me think about it."

"Thank you, my friend," Greene responded. With that, he left the Geiger home. Emily followed.

"General," she began, "I can do it. Take the message for you."

Greene looked at her skeptically. "I know you mean well, but this is dangerous. You would be risking your life."

"I would probably be safer than a man. After all, who would suspect me? If stopped, I can say I am going to visit my Uncle Jacob. His place is not too far from there."

The general remained silent for a moment. *Could such a young girl travel through that difficult area?* Seeing no alternative, he accepted her offer hoping he'd not regret it.

"When can you leave?"

"Dawn," Emily answered.

"Stop by camp when you are ready to go," Greene said, "and I will give you the message for Sumter."

The next morning Emily mounted her horse and rode to meet the general.

"This note explains that the British plan to abandon the fort. Sumter should bring his troops to Orangeburgh, South Carolina, immediately. Together we can defeat Rawdon," he said sealing the note. "Do not tell anyone. You will be going through areas crawling with British soldiers and sympathizers. They cannot get their hands on this."

"I understand, sir. I won't let you down."

"Emily, this is extremely dangerous. I'll understand if you want to reconsider."

"My father would go if he could," she responded, lifting her chin. "I will go in his place."

Taking the note, she mounted her horse and began her journey. The first day she struggled through several of the South Carolina swamps without encountering any Tories or British. After an exhausting day of riding, she stopped at the house of the relative of a friend. Stating that she was on her way to see her uncle who was ill, she asked to spend the night. She had stayed there on other occasions so was invited inside. The host couple was friendly, but Emily worried they suspected her story was untrue. Before the others woke, she left a note stating she wanted an early start. Then Emily stole out of the house, led her horse away from the buildings, and continued on her journey.

It was on the second day that the British scout intercepted her near the Congaree River.

Now, in custody, her mission was in jeopardy. She fought to remain calm, but fear gripped her heart. Had her luck run out? This could spell disaster for General Greene—and her.

Emily paced the room. What should she do? How could she protect the letter? The room was small, barren. No cubbies, no loose floorboards. Nowhere to hide it. She feared discovery. Her mind raced. *Think, Emily. There has to be a something you can do. They can't find the message. Think.*

Suddenly, she knew. Retrieving the note, she memorized each word. When she could repeat it exactly, she ripped the letter into small bits. Shoving the shredded paper into her mouth, she put her plan in motion. The dry paper stuck in her throat. She chewed and swallowed piece after piece, gagging down every morsel. Her heart felt lighter with each swallow.

Several minutes later, the British brought in an older Tory woman to search Emily. When finished, she went into the hallway to report to Rawdon, leaving the door ajar. Emily listened, anxious to hear her fate.

"I found nothing," the woman said.

"Are you sure? Were you thorough? Did you check everywhere?" the officer asked.

"Yes. I examined the girl. I even checked the hems and looked for secret pockets. Nothing."

"Thank you," he replied.

Suspicions relieved, Rawdon knocked on the door and entered. He apologized for detaining her and told her she was free to leave.

A soldier brought her horse to her and she rode from the British fort, taking a roundabout route toward her destination. It was important to take every precaution. She knew she could not withstand another interrogation.

After several hours, she arrived at General Sumter's camp.

"I need to see the general," she said. "It is important. I have a message for him."

"What is this concerning?"

"My message is for General Sumter only. Please. He needs to know this."

The soldier hesitated but led her to Sumter.

"General Greene sent me. He gave me a message for you."

"General Greene? That is quite a distance. The British are all around," Sumter stated.

"Yes, sir. They stopped me and searched me."

"They searched you? They found the message?"

"No, sir," Emily said with pride. "I swallowed it."

"You *swallowed* it?" Sumter repeated, shaking his head and staring at the girl in front of him.

"Yes. I tore it into bits and ate it."

"So, Greene's message is lost," he sighed.

"No, sir. I memorized it first. I can tell you every word."

After she relayed the specifics of General Greene's plan, General Sumter gathered his troops and they marched to Orangeburgh, South Carolina.

The reinforced Continental Army engaged the enemy at Eutaw Springs near the Santee River. The battle lasted several hours, with both sides suffering heavy losses. Although not a total victory for the Patriots, the British retreated from the area. This turned out to be the last major battle in the South during the American Revolution.

* * * * *

The Cayce Historical Museum in Cayce, South Carolina, honors Emily and her bravery. The museum itself is a replica of Fort Granby. One of the displays shows a mannequin of Emily waiting upstairs for the matron to search her. In addition, a plaque stands outside the museum describing her heroism on July 3, 1781.

CHAPTER FOUR

I Can Fight as Well as Any Man

Pennsylvania, 1777

Anna Maria Lane ran her fingers through her hair wondering what the day would bring. Within minutes, her husband, John, entered their tent.

"Sounds like the British are about fifteen miles away," John said, embracing her. "We're movin' out shortly."

Anna Maria breathed deeply. Pulling herself free, she adjusted her britches and grabbed her hat. "Ready."

"You don't need to come. We were lucky last time. No one figured out your secret," her husband said. "It's gonna be a long march. Not sure what we'll face. Maybe you should stay behind."

"No," she replied. "We need soldiers; anyone who can fight. I can fight as well as any man. I can keep up with you and the rest. I'm comin'."

"You don't have to prove anything to me. I want you safe." Her husband outlined her chin with his fingers. Her eyes met his.

"We're in this together. This is our lives, our future. I am *not* stayin' behind," Anna Maria said moving back slightly.

"Well, best be goin' then," John relented, shaking his head.

The couple joined the rest of their unit and listened to instructions.

"We'll march to Germantown tonight," General Putnam explained. "Howe and his men are camped there. Hopefully, we'll surprise them. It'll be a long haul. No talking. No noise. Step softly. We strike at dawn. May God watch over us."

The Lanes' unit started out. Anna Maria tugged at her hat to cover her face. She had started as a camp follower, washing clothes, cooking, helping where needed. But when it looked as though John and the others would be gone for weeks or months, she knew she couldn't stay behind. Fear for him would consume her. She had made up her mind. She could shoot. She was strong. She'd disguise herself and fight with the men. Now, enmeshed with the Patriots, she hoped not to be discovered or she'd be ridiculed and thrown out. Or worse. She lowered her head.

They marched on. Nearing the enemy encampment, Anna Maria wondered about tonight's mission. What was ahead? Was theirs the only unit advancing? How many British troops would they face? She'd know soon enough.

Earlier, Anna Maria had seen General George Washington ride into camp and meet with his commanders. She knew Washington—and all the Patriots—yearned for a victory. The British had captured Philadelphia, the colonial capital. American troop morale was low. If the Patriots could win one battle, maybe more, that would lift their spirits and swing momentum to the Continental Army. She wondered how Washington planned to achieve this goal.

From what Putnam had revealed to their unit, Washington hoped to attack the British troops camped in Germantown, about five miles out of Philadelphia. The assault would come from different sides, a synchronized surprise attack. The details, though, were not known to her.

She and the others marched on through the darkness and fog. The cool, moist air enveloped them making vision difficult and creating an eerie feeling. Anna Maria could feel the tension among the men. While the conditions helped hide them, it also slowed their travel due to uncertainty of directions. They stumbled through darkness striving to maintain their course. One unit lost its way and fell behind, missing the entire battle.

Communication broke down between the American generals. Each unit felt isolated from the others. Chaos resulted. Instead of a synchronized hidden advance, British guards detected the enemy approach and pickets alerted their army. The Americans found themselves fighting before they had planned.

Unsure of where to attack, some Patriot troops panicked and retreated. Others fired wildly, hitting their own soldiers. Cries of "I'm out of ammunition" or "My powder is gone" added to the pandemonium. Fearing that their comrades could not fire on the British, some men dropped their weapons and ran. Anna Maria witnessed many scrambling blindly from the action, pushing others out of the way. Frozen momentarily, she wondered what to do.

Furious, the American generals ordered the troops to charge. Commands sounded throughout the air.

"Forward, forward," they shouted as they galloped among men waving their swords. "Push them back…remember the cause…don't give up. Charge!"

The most courageous Patriots followed their generals into battle. Others ran from the fight with fear on their faces. Amidst the bedlam, Anna Maria stood her ground, returning British gunfire. She refused to retreat. She charged forward, musket at hand. Through the gun smoke and fog, she saw her husband, musket to his shoulder, in the fray. Seeing his determination steeled her resolve to continue.

Again and again, the Patriots tried to overtake the enemy who sought refuge in a large stone house called the Chew house, which was owned by Chief Justice Benjamin Chew. Each time the British fired upon the advancing Americans, forcing them to retreat. The rebels persisted, regrouping and charging again. But as the Patriots approached, a volley of gunfire greeted them. Bullets claimed soldiers on both sides. The roar of muskets and cries of soldiers in pain filled the battlefield. With a final surge, the Americans pushed into the house. Hand-to-hand combat ensued with some battling in the home and others spilling outside into the yard. Eventually, the British proved too much for the disorganized rebels, who started to withdraw.

Then, it happened. Anna Maria cried out, grabbing her thigh as a bullet coursed through her, splintering bone. She crumpled to the ground, blood soaking her britches and darkening the ground around her. In the melee, no one noticed her. Unsure if she could survive, she determined to fight to the end. Propping herself up against a tree, she turned back to the battle. Loading and firing, she provided cover for her retreating comrades. At least she could continue to aid the Patriots.

Suddenly, arms pulled at her, dragging her into a bloody ditch. She turned to see John at her side with a look of relief on his face.

"When I saw you fall, I was afraid…" John began.

Anna Maria squeezed his arm. "I'll be fine with you to help me."

"Can you walk? Lean on me."

"I'll manage. Drag me if you must."

Together, the couple struggled out of the ditch and met up with their troop as the Americans retreated. The British pursued them for a few miles, but eventually stopped, satisfied that they held Germantown.

Exhausted from the five-hour battle, the rebels returned to camp. Anna Maria and her husband found a private area away from the others. They embraced for a few silent moments, grateful to have survived.

Anna Maria grimaced in pain as John examined her wound.

"This isn't good. You need a doctor."

"No," she insisted. "Cut the bullet out. I'll be fine."

"I don't know how to remove it. I don't want to lose you."

"We can't risk it. I'll heal and fight again."

Anna Maria took her husband's hand and looked into his eyes.

"Together, we can do this, John. I know we can."

John breathed deeply and nodded. He cleaned his knife as well as possible and began. Gently he probed the knife tip into the wound, searching for the bullet. Anna Maria struggled to suppress her agonized cries as the primitive surgery continued. Sweat poured over her. Each minute felt like hours to her until she heard John's words.

"I got it. I got it. The worst is over," John promised. "I'll bandage it. You rest now."

Anna Maria managed a weak smile as he kissed her forehead.

Although John removed the bullet, the wound never fully healed. It bothered Anna Maria for the rest of her life. True to her word, she remained by her husband's side throughout the war. She continued marching and fighting together with her comrades.

While the Americans did not win the Battle of Germantown,

they fought valiantly. Despite the confusion, they reorganized and battled again, surprising the British with their fierce determination. This lifted the American troops' morale and gave them confidence in their abilities and that of their leaders.

* * * * *

After the war, the Lanes lived in Virginia where John worked for the state arsenal in Fluvanna County. In 1801, they moved to Richmond, Virginia. John worked for the Public Guard and Anna Maria assisted in a military hospital. Several years later, she stopped working due to her health. While at this hospital, a doctor noted her disability.

"What caused your limp?" he inquired.

"Well, I guess I can tell now. I fought against the British," she explained. "The Redcoats got me at Germantown."

"You fought? But, you're…"

"A woman," she said. "During the war, I hid it from everyone. We needed every soldier. Every rifle. I had to stay. It gave me a bad leg, but I'm proud of what I did."

Moved by her story, the doctor appealed to the state of Virginia to consider issuing a pension to her for her valiant service.

On January 28, 1808, Virginia's Governor William H. Cabell sent a letter to the Speaker of the House of Delegates on behalf of soldiers who fought in the Revolutionary War. In his letter, he specifically mentioned Anna Maria Lane stating she was "very infirm, having been disabled by a severe wound which she received while fighting as a common soldier, in one of our Revolutionary battles, from which she never has recovered, and perhaps never will recover."

The House agreed. In 1808, while awarding seven male soldiers an annual pension of $40, the House awarded Anna Maria, Virginia's only known female American Revolution soldier, an annual pension of $100 citing her wound and heroism at the Battle of Germantown.

She died two years later.

CHAPTER FIVE

The Quaker Spy

Pennsylvania, 1777

Lydia Darragh crept down the hallway of her Philadelphia home, taking care not to wake her husband or children. What would she do if discovered? How could she explain her defiance of Major Andre's order to stay in her room? Thoughts and fears raced through her mind, but she steadied herself and tiptoed toward her goal. She was certain the British officers were planning something of great importance. What was it? She needed to find out. There was no turning back as she reached the parlor door.

According to the British Quartering Act, colonists were

required to house and feed British troops as well as provide forage for their horses. The colonists had no choice but to accommodate British needs. While the Darraghs remained in their house, the British often used their parlor for meetings. When Major John Andre of the British Army told Lydia they would be using the room that evening, it wasn't unusual. But Andre's insistence that the Darragh family go to bed early and stay in their rooms concerned her. He emphasized that no one in the house be outside of the bedrooms. *This was no ordinary meeting.* Lydia had to find out what they were doing. Why did the British insist that no one be awake?

Once in place, she strained to hear the conversation in the parlor. She stood perfectly still, held her breath, and listened intently. Bits and pieces of conversation were audible, "*surprise attack…Washington…two days.*" Leaning in closer, she heard more.

"We'll attack Whitemarsh in two days," General William Howe of the British Army stated. "Any questions?"

"What should we tell the troops?" someone asked.

"Surprise is the key," Howe answered. "For now, tell no one. We'll wait to the last minute to reveal the plan. The fewer who know, the better our chances to catch those rebels off guard. They won't stand a chance."

Lydia's heart raced at Howe's words, realizing the implications. Her son, Charles, was in Whitemarsh. He and the others would be slaughtered. She needed to warn him.

From the other side of the wall, chairs scraped against the floor, voices trailed off, and footsteps sounded. The meeting was breaking up. Lydia retreated to her room. She lay quietly in her bed, her heart racing. Her thoughts spun around. What should she do?

After several minutes, there was a soft knock on her door. Lydia didn't respond. Again, a knock disturbed the silence. Holding her breath, she stayed still. Then a third knock, more forceful. Slowly, she crossed the room and opened the door slightly, yawning as though waking from a sound sleep.

"I'm sorry to disturb you," Major Andre apologized. "We've finished our business. You can close up the house."

"Of course," Lydia replied, yawning again. "I'll douse the fire and take care of things. Good night, Major."

"Good night."

Lost in her thoughts, Lydia completed her tasks. She wrestled with her conscience all night. She and her family were Quakers and, according to their beliefs, they were to remain neutral with concerns of war. While she sympathized with the Patriots and believed they had a right to independence, aiding one side or another could result in sanctions from her church, possibly excommunication. Her son, Charles, had broken away from the Quaker beliefs, joining the Second Pennsylvania Regiment. Lydia debated if she also could defy her religion and warn her son. She agonized over what to do.

Arguing with herself, she finally determined that she *had* to pass on what she learned. But, how could she get the message to General Washington and his army? This was going to be difficult, but it was imperative that she relay this information as quickly as possible. She went to bed weighing her options. Finally, she knew what to do.

When morning came, she put her plan in motion. Time was of the essence. Lydia scribbled a note and thrust it in her pocket. Grabbing an empty flour sack, she hurried to the British headquarters.

"Good morning," Lydia greeted the soldiers.

"Good morning, ma'am. What can I do for you?" the British officer asked.

"I'm running low on flour. May I have a pass to go to the flourmill?"

"Of course," the officer replied, signing his name and handing the pass to her.

Lydia thanked him and continued on her way. Instead

of going directly to the mill, she set out to find a way to relay the information to General Washington. Whom could she trust with this sensitive information? If it fell into the wrong hands, her fellow Quakers might sanction her, but that wasn't the only punishment she might face. The act of treason was bound to bring other consequences to her and possibly her family.

What if I'm caught? I'm endangering William and the children. They're innocent. But, I can't just forget about Charles and the others. I have to warn them.

She traveled farther looking for the right person. Eventually she met an American sympathizer who was also a family friend.

"Please," she pleaded, pressing the note into his hand, "deliver this to General Washington."

"Where did you get this?" he asked, studying the message.

"I can't explain…just please. It's true. Just don't tell anyone it was me…my family can't be involved. But Washington must know."

After he reassured her, Lydia hurried on her way. She returned to the flourmill, filled her order, and set out for home, relieved that she managed to pass on the warning. She only hoped the message would get through in time. All that was left now was to wait and see what would happen. While she tried to continue her normal daily routine, her thoughts drifted to the fate of her son and the other soldiers. *Did they receive the message? Did they believe her? Would Charles be safe?*

On December 4, 1777, Lydia watched the British troops march out of Philadelphia toward Whitemarsh. She silently prayed her efforts had not been in vain. Could the Patriots really defeat the British if they attacked? What would happen to her son and the others? The British greatly outnumbered the Continental troops, but Lydia had warned them so the element of surprise shouldn't be a factor. Hopefully, her actions would keep them safe.

Several days later, the British troops returned, quiet and subdued. There had been no surprise attack, but rather the militia had been fully prepared for the enemy. When Washington had learned of the plan, he turned his attention to Whitemarsh. His leadership skills reaped rewards. There had been some fighting but no decisive victory. The planned attack was a total failure. The British troops marched back demoralized.

Throughout the town, Lydia heard the rumors that the British believed that a spy had revealed their plans. No one seemed to know exactly who was suspected, and no names were given. Fear gripped her as she wondered if her involvement would come to light. *Do they know what I did? Do they suspect me? Have I endangered my family?* She prayed not.

Several days later there was a knock on the Darragh door. When Lydia answered, she found herself face-to-face with Major Andre.

"Madam, I need to speak to you."

"Of course," Lydia answered, hiding her trembling hands. "Come in."

"The other night when we met in the parlor, I instructed you to send your family members go to their rooms and to stay there."

"Yes, I remember."

"Did your husband or any of your children leave their rooms at all while we were here?" He looked her squarely in the eye as he spoke.

"No, sir. My family members did exactly as instructed." Lydia met his gaze.

"You're sure? Think carefully."

"Yes, I'm sure. They did not leave their rooms."

"Very well. I know you also stayed in your room as it took several attempts to waken you. Yet, one thing is certain. Someone told the enemy of our meeting. Our plan was foiled and we looked like fools. The walls must have ears."

Andre left the house and Lydia closed the door. She leaned against it and steadied her breathing. *I answered truthfully. William and the children did not leave their rooms.*

Later, Lydia learned the impact of her message. Because of the warning, the Patriots created a ruse to mislead the British. General Washington, knowing the enemy outnumbered his troops, tricked them. He brought in additional troops and immediately ordered his men to spread out and light more campfires than necessary to create the illusion that there were more troops than actually existed. Seeing what they believed to be a large number of reinforcements of the militia, the British decided their plan would not succeed. Instead of a full-out attack, they engaged in small skirmishes. Frustrated, they retreated and returned to Philadelphia admitting failure. The British left Philadelphia in 1778.

* * * * *

Lydia did not reveal her role to anyone else until after the war. If discovered earlier, she would certainly have been charged with treason and possibly executed. She risked these consequences but protected her family. Lydia defied the

Quakers' firm belief to remain neutral in times of war, which must have been a difficult decision. She set aside her beliefs, saving the Whitemarsh soldiers from certain defeat.

In 1783, William Darragh died. Lydia continued to live in their home for three more years, then purchased a new house and operated a store. She quietly lived out the rest of her life as an uncelebrated hero, dying in 1789 at the age of 61.

CHAPTER SIX

Alias Bobby Shurtleff

New York, 1782

Smoke from the battle lingered over the bloodstained ground. The Patriots searched through the bodies for any living being. Moans brought them to one of their own, wounded, but breathing.

"Here," one called. "I found another, still alive."

Others swarmed to the site. "It's Bobby," one said. "Bobby Shurtleff."

"Just leave me," the soldier pleaded. "Let me die. Just go."

His blood soaked clothes and a deep gash on his forehead concerned those who found him. They worried over the severity of his wound and felt he was rambling from loss of blood. He couldn't *want* to be left behind. Even if the enemy didn't return to finish him off, he would not last long in his condition.

"We aren't far from the doctor's tent, and he can help you. We'll get you there, Bobby," they insisted.

"No, I'll only slow you down. Just go."

Against the protests of their injured comrade, the men lifted him gently and placed him on a horse. Guiding the horse, they sought help for their friend and the other wounded. The country terrain was rough and rugged, but the group eventually reached their destination.

Once at the camp, Robert Shurtleff grimaced as the doctor tended to the gash on his head. Eyeing the young soldier, he cleaned and sewed the wound.

"Looks like you lost a lot of blood. Let's see where else you are hurt," the doctor said, putting his hand on Robert's shoulder.

"Just my head," Robert claimed, moving away a bit. Noticing the look of doubt from the doctor, he continued, "There were many wounded on the field. I crawled across them to get to cover. Most of the blood is theirs."

He then described a skirmish with some Loyalists on that summer day in 1782.

"We came across a group of Tories and British. They put up quite a fight and we lost some men but we pushed 'em back. Then we rested near Tappan Zee. But another group ambushed us, and I got this," Robert recalled, pointing to his forehead. "Bodies everywhere, ours and theirs."

His account was true but he had left out some details. It was during the first skirmish that Robert received his head wound, a souvenir from a British saber. Afterwards, he tended the wound himself, but it reopened after the second skirmish. During the second day's battle, Robert was also shot in the thigh. Most of the blood covering his body and uniform belonged to him, not others. But he hoped the doctor believed otherwise.

Injured soldiers moaning in pain lay strewn throughout the makeshift hospital. Robert lucked out. Another soldier's cries demanded the immediate medical attention of the doctor. When the surgeon turned his back, Robert grabbed some supplies, slipped out of the tent and limped away. If he stayed any longer, the doctor might probe further. He couldn't risk that. The soldier needed to get as far away as possible before discovery of his secret.

In reality, Robert Shurtleff was Deborah Samson, a young woman from Massachusetts who impersonated a man so she could join the army. She feared discovery more than death. If anyone knew her identity, the army could throw her out of her unit and subject her to scorn and humiliation. She could never show her face again, and her deceit would never be forgiven. Just thinking of that made her shiver. She hobbled away seeking a deserted area to tend her wound without interference.

Using her penknife as a scalpel, Deborah probed for the musket ball in her thigh. Pain ripped through her, but she prodded the blade deeper, determined to remove the offending object. Wooziness and nausea overwhelmed her, but she continued. Again and again, she maneuvered the blade inside her wound without success. Wiping sweat from her brow, she stuffed a rag into her mouth to stifle her screams. Where was that musket ball? She *had* to remove it! Taking a deep breath, she twisted and turned the knife searching for it. This time, success! Using the tip, she outlined the orb and wrapped her fingers around it.

Finally, she thought as she exhaled. With a sense of relief, she collapsed for a moment. Then she bandaged the wound. Breathing deeply, she closed her eyes to rest for a while. After a time, Deborah woke. Forcing herself to stand, she hobbled toward the rest of her military unit. If questioned, she would simply state she was sore and tired from the battle.

She should have rested longer to allow time to heal but felt a sense of obligation to join her comrades as soon as possible. As a result, her leg never mended completely. It troubled her throughout the rest of her life.

The self-surgery, though, served its purpose. She kept her identity a secret. None of her companions realized the truth about Deborah. She had entered the Fourth Massachusetts Regiment of the Continental Army by pretending to be male and using the name of Robert Shurtleff. As far as the other soldiers were concerned, she was simply "Bobby" who fought courageously in battle. They had no idea they fought side-by-side with a woman.

Over the next few days, Deborah thought about her secret. She recalled an earlier attempt to enlist in the army under a different name. Dressed in men's attire, she had approached the recruiters.

"I'm here to volunteer for service," she had said.

"Name?" the recruiter asked.

"Timothy Thayer."

"Can you shoot?"

"Yes."

"Sign here. Make your X if you can't sign," the recruiter

said, sliding a paper in front of her. Chatter filled the room behind Deborah as she nodded.

While she signed, another man had approached, looking closely at Deborah. He circled her, studying her.

"I know you. You aren't Timothy Thayer," the man accused. He turned to the recruiter, "This here's a woman. Deborah Samson. She used to work for a farmer up the road."

Deborah had looked up and into the accusing eyes of a neighbor. Blushing, she tried to turn away.

The recruiter jumped up, overturned his chair, and confronted Deborah. "Is this true? Are you a woman?"

The recruiting station went silent and Deborah felt everyone watching. She nodded, saying nothing.

"Get out of here!" he had shouted, grabbing the papers and ripping them. "Stop wasting our time and don't ever return. If you do, I'll see you jailed!"

Feeling shame and humiliation, she had left the room, giving up her plan.

However, her desire to aid the Patriots had been too great. She felt a calling to fight for her new country on the front line of the action. There *had* to be a way to join the Continental Army and serve her country. Summoning all her courage, she waited a month, walked to a neighboring community, and enlisted using the name of Robert Shurtleff. This time she succeeded. In 1782, the Fourth Massachusetts Regiment of the Continental Army welcomed the new recruit. She had reached her goal.

Deborah's childhood had been difficult. Her father left the family when she was five years old, and her mother struggled to care for her and her siblings. Out of desperation, her mother sent Deborah away and the young girl ended up working in several homes as an indentured servant, a common practice during this time. Her duties had included tending crops, milking cows, and hauling firewood. The heavy lifting of rural life strengthened her physically and emotionally. Hard work became a part of her daily routine and aided her future disguise.

Since she was taller than most women, and many men, she could pass as a male. Her broad shoulders and strong muscles worked to her advantage, and her frame was consistent with most farmers of that time. No one questioned her gender.

Marching next to the men in her regiment, she never complained. She didn't falter as she practiced and drilled with them while carrying her equipment. She volunteered for duties that required strength and courage. The lack of food and constant marching did not discourage her. She fought in skirmishes and endured the same harsh conditions as other soldiers. Her fellow comrades were proud to have Bobby at their side.

Being extremely cautious, Deborah immersed herself in the role of "Robert." She slept in her uniform as all soldiers did, taking every precaution not to be discovered. The young soldier seldom bathed, and when she did, she bathed in the dark of night. Keeping her secret was always foremost in her mind. Even when exhausted from the physical work, she never let down her guard.

Since Deborah took care of her leg herself, no one else was aware of that injury. As far as others were concerned, the only injury to the soldier was the head wound. Because of that, the army pronounced her fit enough to rejoin her unit before her leg fully healed. She continued to serve her country until her luck ran out in July of 1783.

The army sent her unit to Philadelphia that summer. At that time, a dangerous fever hit many people, including Deborah. The illness got the best of her, and she fainted. Her comrades once again came to her rescue and carried her to the hospital for treatment. The attending physician, Dr. Barnabas Binney, examined the sick soldier and discovered her secret.

"Soldier, I know you are not who you say you are," he said.

"Please," Deborah pleaded, "don't say anything. I'll

be thrown out of the army. I just wanted to fight for our country. And I *did* fight for our country. I did everything I could. Please."

"I can't ignore this, but I have no desire to embarrass you. I'll see what I can do and I'll plead your case."

Dr. Binney quietly revealed Deborah's identity to her superiors. He explained her contributions to America. He emphasized that she was wounded while fighting valiantly. The officers chose to treat the young soldier with understanding and compassion.

After nearly two years of disguising herself, "Robert" once again became "Deborah." The young woman returned to Massachusetts in October of 1783 after the army honorably discharged her. In 1785, she married Benjamin Gannett, and they had three children.

While it took several years, her country recognized her service and bravery, and she received a soldier's pension for her service. She later toured the country speaking about her time as Robert Shurtleff and often wore her uniform while doing this. Instead of hiding her identity, Deborah now proudly proclaimed her gender and her accomplishments as a soldier in the Continental Army.

She died at the age of 66.

CHAPTER SEVEN

Secret Codes and Petticoats

New York, 1778

Cautiously, Anna Smith Strong made her way to the clothesline. Picking up her laundry one piece at a time, she shook them out and hung them to dry. Her hands trembled as she arranged each item. She prayed she would not be detected and strived to look as normal as possible.

While it appeared that Anna was simply doing her laundry, she was actually sending information to her neighbor, Abraham Woodhull. He was in charge of the day-to-day operations of the Culper Spy Ring, also known as the Setauket Spy Ring, on Long Island. But if the British suspected

Anna's true purpose, they would arrest her, imprison her, and charge her with treason, possibly even sentence her to death. Despite this, she signaled her neighbor.

General George Washington had appointed Benjamin Tallmadge, a young officer in the Continental Army, to establish a spy ring to operate behind enemy lines on Long Island. Tallmadge, from Setauket, enlisted a handful of his most trusted friends for this assignment. Woodhull, a farmer who lived next to Anna, was one. In turn, Woodhull approached Anna about helping him.

"I don't know," she had said. "It's so risky."

"Just let me know when Brewster is in the area," Woodhull insisted, referring to Caleb Brewster, a trusted friend and another member of Culper's Spy Ring. "You can recognize his boat. Let me know when you see it and where it is."

She shook her head. "It's too dangerous. People would wonder why I constantly visit you. They'd talk. We'd be watched."

"No, I can see your property from my place. We'll set up some kind of signal. That will cut down on any visits."

"I don't know…"

"Just think about it. Or think about Selah and what they did to him," he said, referring to Anna's husband, who had been imprisoned on a British ship. "I'll stop by in two days on my way back from town. Promise me you'll consider it."

She nodded.

As Woodhull left, Anna closed her eyes and recalled the past months, the endless days, and the fear-filled nights. Her husband Selah, a Patriot judge, had been arrested in 1778 for treason or "surreptitious correspondence with the enemy." Labeled a traitor, he had been thrown onto a British prison ship, the HMS Jersey, in New York Harbor. Anna knew the unspeakable conditions of the prison ship resulted in the death of many. Her imagination ripped at her.

She yearned to help Selah, see him, comfort him. For months, she had pleaded for permission to visit her husband. Refusal after refusal followed her requests. Finally, Anna was allowed a brief visit. His gaunt face and weakened condition alarmed her. Selah wouldn't last much longer. However, after the first visit, she was allowed to see him on a regular basis, bringing him food and other necessities. Her actions and continued support may have saved his life.

Eventually, Anna convinced her relatives who were British sympathizers to bribe British officials to release her husband. The relatives may have agreed to do this out of love for Anna or sympathy for her young family. Whatever the reason,

Selah received parole and moved to Connecticut to live with other family members. The Strong children accompanied him since it was safer for them there than in New York. He spent the balance of the war there, while Anna remained in Setauket to protect the family property.

Now, as she walked around her land, she considered Woodhull's suggestion. Could she do this? Did she have the nerve? Even if she did, how could she signal him without others recognizing what she was doing? With her mind racing, she looked over the Long Island Sound, studying the boats. Anna knew that Woodhull was right. The location of her property was perfect for this operation. She could easily spot Brewster's boat. But what possible signal could she use? With a sigh, she continued her chores, while mulling things over. All evening it weighed on her mind.

The next morning she started her chores again, sweeping, washing dishes, and moving on to laundry. She hauled it over to her clothesline and looked down at Woodhull's property. Had he thought of an idea? Could there be a signal that wouldn't arouse suspicion? There must be a way! Shaking out her laundry piece by piece, she pinned the items in place. The chore seemed endless. She repeated this task almost daily. Suddenly, she had her answer. Of course!

When Woodhull stopped by as promised, Anna wasted no time in telling him her decision.

"I'll do it."

Woodhull smiled. "I hoped you'd say that. The signal has to be discreet. No one…"

"I know what to do," Anna interrupted. "It's simple, very natural."

"Tell me."

"When I see Brewster's boat in the sound, I'll begin my laundry. I'll hang up one black petticoat—just one—to let you know he's there."

"But, how will I know where he's anchored? There are miles of coastline."

"I thought of that. Look," she said pointing, "see the coves? There are six of them. We'll assign each one a number. I'll hang up the rest of my laundry and randomly insert handkerchiefs throughout the items. The number of handkerchiefs will tell you the cove number. They are so much smaller than other laundry pieces. You should be able to see everything easily from your place."

"That could work," Woodhull said. "But, there's still danger, Anna. The British are looking for Brewster. They know he's been smuggling in goods and they suspect he's spying. Today I heard there's a price on his head. Be careful."

"I will. But, I know in my heart that it's right that I do this."

She watched her neighbor return to his property, her pulse racing. She must never let down her guard.

Anna faithfully watched the sound as she went about her daily chores. The British, though, made her decision to help even more dangerous. Using the power of the Quartering Act, they had moved into the main house on her property, forcing her to move to a smaller cottage. They now *lived* within yards of her. Each day they walked past her and saw her routine.

Despite the daily contact with the British and the fears that she felt, Anna studied the boats as they entered the sound and signaled Woodhull when she saw Brewster's vessel. In turn, Woodhull kept an eye out for the black petticoat. He then rendezvoused with Brewster to transfer information obtained about British movements or plans. Brewster then crossed the waters once more and repeated the secrets to his contact on the other side who notified Washington.

The simplicity of Anna's "laundry code" allowed the Culper Spy Ring to provide important information to Washington and his troops. While the British realized there were spies among the colonists, they never suspected Anna and never caught any member of the Culper Spy Ring.

Despite their apparent success, Anna never let down her guard. Each time she performed this apparently routine chore, her heart pounded, pulse raced, and her palms sweated. Was she being watched? Had anyone figured out the code? Most of her neighbors were British Loyalists who wouldn't hesitate to turn her over to the British if they discovered her role in the spy ring. Yet, she continued. Her loyalty to her friends and allegiance to the Patriots' cause compelled her.

The accuracy and prompt reporting of information by the Culper Spy Ring contributed to Washington and the Continental Army defeating the British and winning the war. The intelligence gathered from this spy ring is also credited with uncovering Benedict Arnold's plot to turn over the fort of West Point to the British—a huge turning point for the Patriots.

After the war, Anna and her husband reunited, lived again in their family home, and raised their nine children. Her spying efforts remained secret from their friends and neighbors long after the war ended.

* * * * *

In 1939, over 160 years after the American Revolution, descendents of one of the spy ring's members discovered letters hidden in an old trunk. These letters revealed the identities of some of the Patriots who comprised the Culper Spy Ring, including Anna Smith Strong.

CHAPTER EIGHT

Dicey's Midnight Swim

South Carolina, 1781

Panic threatened to overtake 15-year-old Dicey (Laodicea) Langston as she swallowed water, gulped for air, and struggled to reach what she hoped was the opposite shoreline of the Tyger River in South Carolina. The river came up to her neck due to heavy spring rains, and the weight of her clothes pulled her down. Icy waters chilled her, but she persisted, wading across the river. She struggled against the raging current, losing her balance several times. Darkness added to the difficulty of her mission. Was she getting closer to the shore? Did she have the strength to make it to the other side?

She pushed herself onward and was rewarded with a glimpse of shoreline. Shivering and dead-tired, she thrashed forward to land.

With a desperate effort, the young woman struggled onto shore. The stillness of the night added to her feeling of loneliness. If only she could catch her breath for a few minutes. Despite her exhaustion, she knew she had no time to waste. She had trudged through the dark of night into South Carolina's wooded areas and swamps and had even forded the river, but resting was not an option. She had to reach her brother, James, and warn him. The Bloody Scouts, a cruel and ruthless group of Loyalists, aimed to track down small bands of militia and destroy them. Right now they were on their way to Little Eden—the site of James' camp. They would show no mercy.

Most of the Langstons' neighbors were Loyalists. Dicey and her family, though, sided with the Patriots. As the young girl went about her daily routine, she often heard her neighbors talking about the war and the rebels. They boasted about the Bloody Scouts and their plans. She managed to ignore them, but the latest information shocked her into action.

"From what I hear," a neighbor had taunted earlier, "it's

just a matter of days before we find your brother and those other traitors. Then we'll take care of 'em. We'll kill 'em all, startin' with your brother."

He had continued to goad her with details that the British knew—the camp location, number of rebels involved, names of who was there.

She had held her tongue but made her decision. She'd sneak out that night while the family slept and find a way to warn James. It was risky, but she had no choice.

It felt like hours until she had heard the steady breathing of her family members. Once she was sure they slept, Dicey acted. She crept out of the house and donned her brother's clothes. The scent from the clothes would allow her to approach James' horse without alarming the animal. The outfit would also disguise her appearance in case someone saw her.

Traveling through fields and forests, she avoided roads and hid among the shadows. She sloshed through marshes and creeks. Desperation gripped her when she came to the banks of the Tyger River and looked down. No bridge, no fallen logs to help her reach the other side. The current raced and Dicey realized it could sweep her away if she lost her footing. She forced herself into the icy waters and waded forward.

Now, tired and cold, the young woman trudged forward, scouring the area for her brother, praying she would be in time. After wandering for over an hour, she located James and his camp. Between tears, words spilled from her mouth.

"James, all of you, leave now," she pleaded. "Cunningham and the Bloody Scouts know where you are, who you are. They're coming here. You'll all be killed. Go, hurry!"

Dicey explained all she had heard. Realizing they were outnumbered, the men decided to leave the area.

Dicey scrounged for provisions and made food for the men to carry. Then she helped them pack, and the militia dispersed throughout the countryside, leaving the camp empty. They had foiled the Bloody Scouts' plan.

Once the men were safely on their way, Dicey began her perilous trip home. Avoiding roads and trails again, she prayed she wouldn't be detected. What possible excuse could she give for being out at this time of night, in the area of the rebel camp? None. The enemy would be merciless if they discovered her.

She imagined the Bloody Scouts' reaction when they found no one at the camp and realized their prey had escaped. They would be fuming at the lost opportunity. Who had warned them? Where had they gone? Frustrated, they'd be forced to give up their pursuit—at least for now.

Dicey's bravery was even more remarkable considering that she and her father, Solomon Langston, had previously been warned about aiding the rebels. Their neighbors suspected she had passed on information about troop movements to her brother on other occasions. Several times they saw her returning from the direction of an enemy encampment. They had confronted her at home in front of her invalid father.

"Where've you been?" one of the men had demanded.

"Out walkin'."

"Well, if you're goin' to see your rebel brother, you'll be sorry. He's a traitor. If you help him, you're a traitor, too."

"I'll do what I want!" Dicey had retorted.

"You won't live long if you continue."

"You don't scare me," the girl had answered. "I'm free to do as I please."

"Well, what about your ol' father here?" one Tory had threatened, pointing his pistol at the crippled man.

"No," Dicey had shouted, throwing herself in front of her father. "Leave him alone!"

"Traitors need to be dealt with."

"I won't go again. I'll stop. I promise."

"Just remember. If you break that promise, we'll be back."

With that, the men had left. Her father begged her not to go back on her promise, saying he couldn't bear to lose her. She had agreed.

This memory had weighed heavily on Dicey's mind when she left tonight to warn the militia. She couldn't be seen and she'd needed to travel in the cover of darkness. It was important that her father know nothing of her actions. He had done nothing wrong. If she were caught, what would happen? Still, she knew she had to act.

When the teenager returned home after warning her brother about the Bloody Scouts, she continued to be cautious. She snuck in without waking anyone, arose the next morning with the rest of the family, made breakfast, and continued her regular routine. No one knew of her involvement. Her secret remained within her heart. But a slip of the tongue would endanger everyone she loved. Too high of a price.

While her neighbors may have suspected her participation, they failed to uncover her role that night. Nothing pointed to Dicey. In true heroic form, she quietly protected her father, her family, and herself from any retaliation.

In 1783, Dicey married Thomas Springfield, whom she'd met during the war. Thomas, who served with James, had come to the Langston home claiming James sent him to pick up a gun. Dicey had gone into the house to retrieve it. She paused remembering that James had left instructions that if someone came for it, the messenger needed to give a code word or signal. Weapons were extremely valuable during this time and often stolen. Just as she held out the gun, Dicey recalled her brother's words. She aimed the gun at Thomas, cocked it, and demanded the code or signal. Thomas stated she must be James' sister to have such a daring attitude. He then repeated the secret code and received the gun.

He returned to court her after the war. They married in 1783 and Dicey gave birth to 22 children.

Dicey died in 1837 at the age of 71 and was buried in the family cemetery.

Just north of Traveler's Rest, South Carolina, stands a marker erected by the Daughters of the American Revolution honoring "Daring Dicey."

Chapter Nine

There Goes My Petticoat

New Jersey, 1778

Mary Ludwig Hays wiped the sweat from her brow as she trudged through the New Jersey battlefield on June 28, 1778. Temperatures topped 100 degrees and warmth radiating from the artillery added to the uncomfortable conditions. Heat and smoke made breathing difficult. Parched throats. Burning eyes. Soldiers and others on both sides succumbed to heat exhaustion as the battle raged.

"Here! Over here!" a gunner called, waving his arms.

Mary made her way to the man. She pushed a water pitcher at him. "Drink this."

He gulped. "Thanks. Pour some on the cannon to cool it down."

She did as requested, and the soldier swabbed out and reloaded his cannon, firing again. Smoke billowed over the field. Mary scanned the area, ran down the hill toward the creek, pitcher in hand. Refilling it, she returned to the men, bringing water to those in need. No shortage of work. The battle at Monmouth had been raging for hours.

Mary's husband, William, was an artilleryman with the Fourth Artillery of the Continental Army. When he joined, she decided to accompany him as a camp follower, a term referring to women who followed the army and cooked, washed clothes, sewed, and tended the sick and injured. Due to the British Quartering Act, many women were displaced from their homes. Some wives were reluctant to leave their husbands and felt they could best contribute to the Patriots' cause by being on site. In return for their aid, they received a fraction of the rations provided to the men.

Now, with the Continental Army under heavy fire from the British, Mary and other camp followers did what they could to provide relief for the Americans. From a nearby stream, the women scooped pitchers of water and toted them to the soldiers to quench their thirst and cool the burning-hot artillery. On the field, they nursed the wounded, loaded muskets, and helped swab the cannons.

The work was nonstop and Mary scrambled to keep up. Struggling over the wounded, zigzagging across the battlefield and exposing herself to gunfire, she worked tirelessly. Everywhere she looked, she saw soldiers in need, some writhing in pain, victims of gunfire. Mary knew a number of them would never recover. She yearned to give comfort, and hold them, but knew she couldn't stop to do this. The fighting continued and she was needed elsewhere. No time to rest. She pushed on.

During the battle, Mary scanned the field wondering where to help next. It was then she saw her husband collapse. William's crumpled body lay on the ground. Fear gripped her. What had happened? Had he been hit? She couldn't lose him!

"William! William, I'm coming," Mary hiked up her skirt and petticoats and hurried to his side. Finding him still alive, she examined him briefly and bathed his face with water. The wound was not serious. He would live. "You'll be all right," she told him

Smoke and sweat burned her eyes as she wiped her face. Seeing the approaching British, she took over her husband's position and helped the crew. Recalling the steps, she seized the rammer to clean the barrel as best she could before others added the powder and cannonball. Helping reposition the cannon toward the enemy, they fired, watching as the shot reached its target. Repeatedly, she executed the steps in unison with the other men.

While Mary worked at the cannon, the enemy fired on her and others around her. At one point, a British cannon ball hurdled through her outstretched legs, shredding her skirt and petticoat. Mary looked down, assessing the damage. She was unscathed.

"There goes my petticoat!" She shrugged. "Well, that could have been worse." She returned to her work at the cannon and continued firing, undaunted by the near miss.

British and Patriots alike were exhausted by day's end. When night fell, the British withdrew. General Washington, seeing them set up camp in the distance, told his troops they would not pursue them in the dark. Instead, he explained they would wait until dawn to attack. But in the morning, he found that the fires and camp had been a ruse. Clinton's army had resumed their march to New York. Washington decided it would be futile to follow and returned to camp.

The Battle of Monmouth was not a decisive victory for either side. The British had been unable to break the lines of the Americans, and the Americans had been unable to overtake the British. Both sides lost hundreds of men. Some died from heat, others from their wounds.

Mary stayed at her husband's station throughout the battle. She never wavered from operating the cannon and helping to fight the British. Many noticed her actions, and her bravery has been recounted many times. The nickname "Molly Pitcher" honors all of the women who helped on the battlefield, but it is closely associated with Mary because of her tireless work at the Battle of Monmouth.

A private in the Continental Army, Joseph Martin, witnessed Mary's close encounter with the cannon ball and wrote about the events in his journal, substantiating her role in the battle.

Mary stayed with her husband and the Continental Army until the end of the war. In 1783, she and William returned to Carlisle, Pennsylvania, where they had previously lived. After William died, she married another army veteran, John McCauley. They lived in Carlisle, where Mary worked at the Pennsylvania State House.

In 1822, the Pennsylvania legislature awarded Mary an annual commission of $40.00. She died on January 22, 1832 and was buried with military honors in Old Carlisle

Cemetery. A white marble monument erected over her grave holds the inscription, "Molly Pitcher, the heroine of Monmouth."

CHAPTER TEN

Knit One, Purl One, Spy on the British

Pennsylvania, 1777

"Good morning, Molly! Going to the ridge?" called a neighbor.

The middle-aged woman waved and nodded to her friend as she continued to her destination, toting her basket.

"It's a great day to lay out my linens," she explained. "They'll bleach, and I'll knit for a while."

She worked her way up the rocky slope and sat on her favorite ledge. It was a rugged climb, but she made the trek often and was used to the uneven ground. She just needed to balance herself and carry her supplies to the top. From the view up there, Molly could see—and be seen—from all directions.

Looking around the valley in Philadelphia, Molly Rinker made herself comfortable. She set her linens to bleach in the sun and prepared to knit. Softly, she muttered, *"Knit one, purl one. Knit one, purl one."* The yarn tickled her hands as she pulled the strands between her fingers. While knitting her pattern, she scanned the area. She knew she could be seen but she was not sure who or how many people saw her.

Appearing to be alone, she "accidentally" dropped a ball of yarn over the edge of the cliff. Just in case someone watched, she shook her head at her clumsiness, hiding a sly smile.

"Molly, Molly, Molly. Be more careful," she admonished herself.

No one who witnessed the scene would suspect her true intent. It looked like an innocent mistake. After all, mistakes happen.

Hidden inside that ball of yarn was information she had uncovered to help the Patriots' cause. Below the cliff, an American courier watched the knitting woman, snatched the yarn, and disappeared into the woods. Once the yarn was unraveled and the message revealed, he took it to General George Washington's camp. The Continental Army welcomed these bits of information, as citizens were often privy to conversations by British officers. This seemingly innocent woman was spying on the enemy and helping the rebels.

Molly hadn't set out to spy or get involved in the war, but recent events forced her to take action. Emotions in Philadelphia ran high. British troops had marched into the city and demanded that colonists house their officers and troops as needed. This Quartering Act upset many people as it left them homeless.

One day, on her way home from purchasing goods, Molly witnessed a British officer confronting her neighbor outside her house. Disturbed by his harsh tone, Molly listened.

"Mrs. Townsend?" the officer had asked.

"Yes, I'm Mrs. Townsend."

"As you know, our army will be staying in Philadelphia. We're in need of housing. Your home is a perfect location to quarter several of our officers. Gather what you need and leave within the hour."

"But where am I to go?" the woman asked. "What am I to do?"

The officer loomed over her. "I'm sure your friends or family can accommodate you. After all, you *do* want to help the *King's officers*, don't you?"

Hearing his words, other neighbors scurried past, avoiding eye contact. Molly, though, slowed her pace, listening.

Mrs. Townsend reddened under his gaze. What could she say? What choice did she have?

"It's j-just that I have small children. Please, m-may I have more time? There is so m-much to do," she begged.

"Very well," he snapped. "Leave by the end of the day."

Turning, he strode away. Molly watched the woman wring her hands then retreat to her home.

The callousness of the act enraged Molly, who vowed to fight back. *Families thrown out of their homes? Women and children left to fend for themselves? This was wrong.* She'd fight back. Under cover of night, she met with a young Patriot and devised a plan to help the rebels by passing along any information she felt might be useful.

From her perch on the rock overlooking Pennsylvania's Wissahickon Valley, Molly had a clear view of the happenings below. She saw the lay of the land as well as British troop movements. This vantage point allowed her to identify when those troops were preparing to move out or when additional troops arrived.

Her knitting excursions were the perfect ruse to monitor

the enemy. She kept track of every detail and wrote the facts on bits of paper at night when she was alone. Then, wrapping yarn around the notes and anchoring them with small stones, she dropped them for the courier. She included the balls of yarn in her basket when she climbed to her post on the ridge. Nothing would look suspicious if the British stopped her to examine the contents of her tote.

This information proved invaluable to the Americans. In particular, a patriotic group, the Green Boys of Roxborough, appreciated this intelligence. They were an elusive guerilla force that disrupted the British and the Hessian mercenaries in the area. The Green Boys raided the enemies' supplies and engaged in skirmishes against small bands of troops to prevent the British from fully focusing on the larger attacks against the Patriots. Knowledge of troop location and movement allowed the guerilla group to avoid detection and continue harassing the enemy.

Molly, often called Mom, also gained additional information by paying attention throughout the day. She owned and operated a tavern in Philadelphia frequented by British officers and soldiers. Because the British viewed women as nonthreatening, they openly discussed their next strategies. The matronly woman took advantage of their mistaken belief. Molly's innocent appearance and demeanor allowed her to overhear chance remarks and details as she moved freely from table to table. Often she heard only bits and pieces.

In particular, Molly helped the Americans with the Battle of Germantown on October 4, 1777. Before the battle, while working in her tavern, she uncovered information concerning the whereabouts and plans of the British troops.

"Where are the other troops going?" one British officer asked.

"Germantown," another responded.

"How many?…General Howe ordered…divide…"

"…8,000…9,000…so rebels can't…"

Molly listened intently. *Was Howe really dividing his troops? Were there 8,000 to 9,000 British troops camped near Germantown?* Another knitting trek verified the facts. Another ball of yarn dropped.

General Washington used this intelligence to determine where and when to attack the enemy. This hard-fought battle showed grit and determination on the part of the Patriots. General John Armstrong of the Continental Army credited Molly's information with preventing the British from wiping out the rebels.

Although the Americans lost this battle, it became a turning point in the war. The fact that the much-outnumbered Patriots fought Sir William Howe and the British so daringly and courageously caught the attention of the French and their foreign minister. France then increased its aid to the struggling Continental Army. The Americans were no longer in this alone. The battle was lost, but not the war.

* * * * *

Today, a ridge at Wissahickon Creek in Philadelphia has been named "Mom Rinker's Rock" in honor of this patriotic spy. This scenic outlook is located at Fairmount Park in Philadelphia where, if you use your imagination, you can see a middle-aged woman sitting, knitting, and spying.

CHAPTER ELEVEN

Martha's Explosive Confession

South Carolina, 1780

Martha Bratton peered through trees and watched Tories and British soldiers march toward her property. She knew they had discovered the location of the hidden gunpowder. They appeared to be on a mission. Closer, closer, heading straight toward the oak tree just as she feared. She needed to act.

Earlier that day, a neighbor had burst into her house.

"Martha, you're in trouble," she had said. "The Tories know you have the gunpowder. They're on their way now to seize it."

"How did they find out?"

Her friend shook her head saying, "I don't know. I just know they're on their way."

"They won't get it," Martha vowed. "I won't let them use it against William and the others."

"They'll be here soon. They aren't far away. You don't have time to move it."

"I can't let it fall into their hands."

"But what can you do?"

"I'm not sure."

"Good luck, Martha. Be careful."

The neighbor had left and Martha had buried her face in her hands debating her options. Governor John Rutledge of South Carolina had encouraged the local Patriots to harass British troops, disrupting their plans. He sent shipments of gunpowder to area militia so they could continue their attacks. The men hid the gunpowder in hollow trees and stumps, or buried it, and even placed it under floorboards in their homes.

When Colonel William Bratton, Martha's husband, received the gunpowder, he concealed it in a hollow oak tree on their property. When he left to fight with the Patriots, he revealed the hiding place to his wife, stressing that she could not let the enemy confiscate it. Martha willingly assumed the responsibility, promising to keep the precious commodity out of the hands of the British.

These thoughts swirled in Martha's mind as she watched the enemy advance. Within minutes, they would recover the gunpowder unless she took action. She knew what she must do. She sprinted to the hiding place and, breaking open the keg, poured out some of the powder, making a long trail away from the tree. She waited for the British to close in. As the troops approached, she lit the gunpowder, hoping her plan would work. It didn't take long to see the result. The explosion shook the ground, stunning the enemy. The tree demolished. The British sabotaged.

Martha watched. As they stumbled about, the troops appeared confused, dazed, unsure of what had just happened. They scanned the area, looking for rebels. After several minutes, their leader regained his composure and regrouped his men. Following his commands, they marched into town and gathered the townspeople.

"Who is responsible for this?" the officer in charge shouted.

Silence.

"Tell me the name of the man who did this or you will all suffer."

Martha boldly stepped forward. "It was I who did it," she stated. "Let the consequence be what it will." Having been entrusted with keeping the gunpowder safe, she did what she felt was best. But she refused to have an innocent blamed.

Now she stood before the officer awaiting her punishment. He glared at the woman before him.

"*You* blew up the powder? A woman? Or are you covering for someone?"

"It was I and I alone."

"Then you will suffer the consequences. You are confined to your property. You may not leave for any reason." He then described exactly what this meant—no visiting neighbors, no church meetings, no purchasing supplies. She could not step foot off her property.

"But I have a family, children…"

"You should have thought of them before you acted so rashly."

Martha swallowed hard and nodded, angry but determined to face her fate. "For how long?"

"Thirty days. But if you violate this in any way, if you try to help the rebels again, you won't get off so lightly."

Martha served her sentence but was more determined than ever to help the Patriots. Whenever she heard her husband's unit was close, she would send them information about British troop movements or actions by Loyalist neighbors, helping the rebels sabotage the enemy.

With this harassment of their troops, the British ordered units of men to destroy those small bands of attackers. They searched the countryside and raided homes looking for Patriots to arrest. Captain Christian Huck led one detachment of British troops assigned to find the rebels. Huck was a particularly brutal man. He bullied his way through the countryside, barging into homes, stealing food, and confiscating horses. He demanded loyalty to Britain and threatened those who opposed him or his efforts.

On July 11, 1780, Huck burst into the Bratton home.

"Where's your traitor husband?" he demanded.

"In Sumter's army," Martha replied, referring to General Thomas Sumter of the Revolutionary Army.

"Where are they hiding?"

"They move around," she answered, shrugging.

Huck decided to try a different approach. He pulled Martha's young son onto his knee.

"It would be a shame for you to be widowed with such a young child to raise. If your husband doesn't surrender, that's what will happen. We'll find him eventually and he'll be hanged. Think about this boy's future without his father. Maybe you could talk to your husband. Convince him he's misguided. He can leave the traitors and join us."

Martha looked Huck in the eyes. "I would rather see him remain true to his duty to his country, even if he perished in Sumter's army."

Outraged, Huck threw the young boy off him and across the room. One of Huck's men jumped up, grabbed a reaping hook and held it against the throat of the woman, threatening to kill her. Despite this treatment, Martha refused to inform on her husband. Captain Huck, angered at her defiance, did nothing to stop the attack or alleviate the tension. Instead, an officer who was second-in-command intervened on her behalf and ordered the soldier to remove the hook, saving her life.

Huck then demanded she prepare food for him and his troops. The woman envisioned adding poison, which she had on hand for pests, but could not bring herself to kill any of these men. She also knew her husband and comrades were in the area. She decided to take another tactic, sending a trusted slave to look for the rebel troops. Maybe they were watching the house and knew Huck was there. Martha prayed this was true.

After eating, the troops, about 115 men, moved a half-mile away to the home of another Patriot, James Williamson. Williamson had a large pasture where their horses could feed and rest. Huck and his men settled in and camped for the night, officers inside the house, troops outside. The stillness lulled them into a feeling of security. Sentries daydreamed or dozed lightly.

Outside the perimeter of the property, Patriot leaders Colonel Bratton and Captain John McClure planned their next move. Martha's messenger had reached them and explained the situation. Seventy-five men waited to hear their orders. While outnumbered, Bratton and McClure knew the enemy was not expecting an attack. They gambled on surprise and darkness to balance the odds. Dividing the troops, the Patriots encircled the property and attacked before dawn. The unsuspecting British and Loyalists scrambled to put up a fight but chaos prevented an organized front.

Twice Huck rallied his troops, but the Patriots controlled the battlefield and the rallies subsided. Soon, Huck and another officer fell in battle. Without leadership, his men gave up and ran off. While some managed to escape, thirty-five Loyalists died, thirty more were wounded, and others were captured and taken prisoner. One Patriot lost his life and another was severely wounded. Others had minor injuries.

The fight had moved toward the Bratton home, and once over, Martha opened her house to the injured, whether friend or enemy. She fed them, tended their wounds, and comforted them. While nursing her patients, the Patriots brought her a prisoner requesting to see her. As an officer leading the Loyalists, they planned to hang him.

"Ma'am, this man requested to see you. Do you know him?"

Martha recognized him as the man who had intervened on her behalf.

"Yes," she nodded. "I know him. He saved my life just a few hours ago. What can I do for him?"

"He is a British officer, ma'am. He is to be hanged for his actions. He requested to see you, first."

Filled with gratitude that he had prevented her certain death, she pleaded that his life be spared.

"No, please, no," Martha said. "He risked retaliation from his own soldiers to save me. Please, don't do this."

"He was leading his men against us. I can't let him go, ma'am," the soldier answered. "You could talk to the captain, but I don't know it will help."

How could she stand by and let him be executed when he

intervened on her behalf? She raced to plead her case to the commanding officer stressing how she would be dead if not for the actions of this British officer. She begged his life be spared. Her request was granted, and the Patriots held him prisoner until an exchange could be made.

The Battle of Huck's Defeat was a rallying point for the militia in South Carolina. The bravery of the Patriots and their desire to fight in this battle encouraged rebellion against British rule. Colonel Bratton continued to lead his men and Martha ran the family farm until the war ended. William died in 1815 and Martha a year later.

* * * * *

Historic Brattonsville in South Carolina is named after this brave family. It includes the original home of the Bratton family, thirty historic buildings, and the site of the battle that raged on that infamous day.

Chapter Twelve

She Ran for Freedom

West Virginia, 1782

The teenager sprinted toward the gates of Fort Henry in West Virginia. Shielding the bundle she carried as best she could, she estimated the distance ahead of her. *Only 70...60...now 50 yards to the fort. I can do this. I will do this,* she vowed. Urgency propelled her as she ran for her life and the lives of everyone in the fort.

Shots surrounded her. Arrows whizzed past. Angry shouts filled the air. Bullets tore through her clothing, yet sixteen-year-old Betty Zane ran forward—determined to deliver her package to those inside the fort. *Should I run in a zigzag pattern?* Rejecting that, she told herself, *don't waste any time. Move on! Get closer! If I fall, maybe I can at least get within reach of the fort. Hopefully, they will send someone out to retrieve the bundle.* The barrage of enemy fire continued as she clamored up the incline. Each step brought her closer to her goal.

The Patriots and settlers inside the fort returned fire at the enemy, hoping to protect the teenager. Holding their breath and praying, they watched Betty's progress. When she reached the fort, they opened the gates. She stumbled inside. Relief, admiration, and disbelief showed on the faces of the fort's occupants, including Betty's brothers, Ebenezer and Silas. How had she managed to reach it unscathed? It was a miracle. Cheers erupted throughout the fort.

Silas ran to his sister. "Are you harmed? Did they hit you?"

"No," she gasped, handing him the package. "I'm not hit."

Betty carried an apron-load of gunpowder into the fort. Without this, the Patriots would have had no chance. Roughly two hundred and fifty Delaware and Wyandot Indians, along with forty British Rangers, laid siege to Fort Henry. They had arrived September 11, 1782, the day before, demanding full surrender of the fort. The Patriots had scoffed at the proposal. The onslaught had begun.

The garrison was almost impenetrable. Built on a hill near the Ohio River, a tall stockade surrounded the building. A catwalk along the inside of the fence provided the occupants a clear view of their attackers. They could hold off the enemy as long as supplies held out. But, their gunpowder supply had dwindled and if the attack continued much longer, Fort Henry would fall to the enemy. Despite their bravado, things looked bleak.

Betty's brother, Ebenezer Zane, knew there was a keg of powder in his cabin halfway down the hill—less than one hundred yards away. If only they could get it! Several men offered to try, but the commander, Colonel David Shepherd, refused.

"We're outnumbered. I can't spare even one man," Shepherd said.

"We need that powder," Ebenezer insisted. "I know I can make it. Let me go."

Shepherd shook his head. "I need you here."

Betty interrupted the men. "I'll do it. The colonel's right, Ebenezer. You'll be killed. I'm a girl. They won't fire on me when I run."

"It's too dangerous," her brother said. "You can't go."

"Let me try. I'm sure I'll make it."

Shepherd hesitated. Could she succeed?

"I'm fast," the girl persisted. "I can do this. You said yourself you can't risk anyone else. Besides, I know exactly where the powder is stored. I won't let you down."

Her brothers argued against it, but Betty reasoned she was the most fleet of foot and also the most expendable. At first, the colonel rejected her offer.

"Your brothers are right. This isn't a job for a young girl."

Betty countered, "Because I'm a girl, I stand a better chance. They're less likely to attack me than an able-bodied man. Plus, every man, every fighter is needed in the fort. Let me go."

Reluctantly, the colonel and others agreed.

The teenager was right. As she ran to the cabin, there were war whoops and calls but no bullets or arrows flew in her direction. She reached her destination without incident. The enemy may have viewed her as harmless, reasoning she merely wanted to get away from the attack on the fort. Why bother with her? What harm could she do?

Once inside the cabin, Betty ran to the corner and pulled at the keg of gunpowder. Too heavy! She couldn't lift it much less carry it. She broke it open, removed her long apron, poured as much powder as she could into it, tied it up, and peered outside. *Would her luck continue? Would they realize what she was doing?* Taking a deep breath, she sprinted from the cabin and ran toward the fort.

This time the enemy recognized something was afoot. What was she doing? Why would she return to the fort? What was she carrying? Within a few seconds, the alarm sounded. Arrows and bullets sprayed around her as she dashed up the hill. Bullets pierced her clothing, but missed her—and the powder. Arrows whizzed past her head, falling nearby. Miraculously, she reached safety and delivered her goods.

With the renewed supply of gunpowder, the Patriots and settlers held off the enemy until reinforcements arrived. The Rangers and Native Americans retreated, abandoning the idea of capturing Fort Henry. This siege, one of the last battles of the Revolutionary War, lasted from September 11-13, 1782.

After the war, Betty married and raised a family near Martins Ferry, Ohio, close to the site of Fort Henry. She died on August 23, 1823, and was buried in Walnut Grove Cemetery in Martins Ferry.

* * * * *

Betty and the Zane family have been memorialized in several ways. The Zane Highway in Eastern Ohio is named after the frontier family. The Betty Zane Room in Wilson Lodge of Oglebay Park in Wheeling, West Virginia, as well as a granite monument to Betty at the entrance of the old Walnut Grove Cemetery, are both named after this heroine. In addition, the well-known author, Zane Grey (descendant of Colonel Ebenezer Zane), penned a fictionalized account of her life in his book titled, *Betty Zane*, published in 1903.

CHAPTER THIRTEEN

The Weight on Her Shoulders

Georgia, 1779

Mammy Kate lifted the wash basket onto her head, shifting it until it felt stable. She stepped forward gingerly, testing the balance. The sun was setting and the air cool, but sweat tickled Mammy Kate's brow and she felt flushed. Ahead the guard waited for her. *Breathe and walk, breathe and walk,* she repeated mentally as she moved forward.

The guard at Fort Cornwallis at Augusta, Georgia smirked. "I don't know why you bother coming here to see him. He don't need no laundry done. We'll soon hang that rebel for being the traitor he is."

"Well," Mammy Kate answered, maneuvering past him and out the gate, "he can at least be wearin' clean clothes when it happens."

The African woman sashayed down the path singing a low song, hoping to appear relaxed. She stood over six feet tall and had incredible strength, but still she strained under the weight of her cargo. Her shoulders and back ached as each step challenged her. Her muscles cried out in pain. With fierce determination, she persevered past several British officers and nearby Tories, careful to keep the basket stable.

Moving out of sight of the fort, she tried to hurry. *Just a few more steps. Keep goin'. Move on.* Her legs protested, burning in agony. Sheer willpower pushed her onward. Finally, convinced she was past the view of the British, and their bullets, she lowered the basket from her head. Pulling the top sheets off, she freed her true cargo—her master, Stephen Heard.

Loyalists had seized Heard after the Battle of Kettle Creek, Georgia, on February 14, 1779. While the Patriots won that battle, the enemy wounded and captured twenty-three Americans, including Stephen Heard. He and the other prisoners were transferred to Fort Cornwallis where they faced charges of treason. As an officer, Heard's penalty was not merely imprisonment. He was to be hanged.

After hearing of her master's captivity, Mammy Kate vowed to free him. He had always treated her and her husband, Daddy Jack, very well.

"I can't sit here and do nothin'," she told Daddy Jack.

"What can *you* do?" her husband asked. "They won't free him jus' cuz you ask."

"I don't know yet. I think of somethin'."

The next morning, she took one of Heard's horses and rode over fifty miles to the fort in Augusta, Georgia. She needed to see her master. In order to do that, she'd have to be allowed visits to the fort. After arriving, she asked to speak to the officer in charge. Explaining her experience with laundry, she offered her services to the British officers and Tories in the area. Her work impressed them and they welcomed her visits. Soon she became a regular.

During one of her trips, she requested to see her imprisoned master, stating she would also do his laundry. The guard shook his head and explained Heard's fate.

"His days are numbered," the guard laughed. "Nobody cares if he's soiled."

"No reason he wear dirty clothes," she insisted. "He can be clean."

"Why bother? He'll be dead soon."

"Clean clothes help everyone," she said. "If he clean, sickness don't spread."

"Fine," the guard replied, "suit yourself. Twice a week. You can see him now."

Mammy Kate entered her master's cell. His gaunt appearance shocked her. He looked so frail, so small. Was he even alive?

"Oh, what they done to you? I got here jus' in time."

"I'm not long for this world," Heard responded. "I know that. Go on. You leave."

"No, sir. Not gonna do that," Mammy Kate insisted. "I be back. You be fine. I find a way to get you outta here."

From then on, she smuggled in food for her master. Often she brought the "Georgia ash cake," a cornbread baked in hot ashes. Since the cake was flat, it was easy to hide inside her clothes. This additional nourishment helped Heard survive.

During each visit, she assured her master she had a plan for escape. She just needed to work out a few details.

Mammy Kate returned several days later and explained her scheme.

"Daddy Jack and me got an idea. I'm strong. I jus' carry you out with the laundry."

"No, you can't do that. I'm touched you want to help, but there's nothing you can do. I'm to be hanged. I know that, I accept that. You go on home, now."

"No, sir. I can do this. I know I can. You're small. You can fit into the wash basket. Jus' try."

Heard followed her instructions. Mammy Kate tucked sheets and other linens around him. She lifted the basket above her and placed it on her head. It took several minutes to stabilize it, but once secure, she proceeded out the front gate.

As part of her plan, Mammy Kate and her husband, Daddy Jack, had hidden two of Heard's Arabian horses in a thicket of woods nearby. She carried her master around a bend in the road out of sight of the fort, lowered the basket, and helped him out.

"Hurry," she urged. "We got horses waitin' for us."

Mammy Kate and Heard raced toward the woods, mounted the horses, and rode off. The guards never saw the laundress or their prisoner again. She had sabotaged their plans.

Once safe, her master turned to Mammy Kate.

"I can't believe you did this. I was headed for the gallows."

"You too good a man to die like that. I had to do somethin'."

"Mammy Kate, I can't thank you enough. You saved my

life. I shall set you and Daddy Jack free. *You're free.* I'll miss you, my friend, but you may go where you want."

"I'm right where I wanna be, takin' care of you and your family. I'm not goin' nowhere," she said raising her chin and scanning the countryside. "This my home. Why I leave my home?"

Despite Heard's arguments, the woman insisted she did not want to go anywhere. Mammy Kate lived the rest of her life as a free woman, but didn't leave the plantation. Heard gave her and her husband a small tract of land there and a four-room house where they raised nine children.

Heard did not return to the Continental Army, but he served in the House of Assembly and eventually became the governor of Georgia. He never forgot Mammy Kate's loyalty. Governor Heard and his family continued to watch over his rescuer. While Heard died without a will, his son, who administered the estate, made sure both Mammy Kate and Daddy Jack were cared for until their deaths.

* * * * *

On October 15, 2011, the Georgia Society of Sons of the American Revolution and the Daughters of the

American Revolution honored Mammy Kate as a patriot of the American Revolution. She was the first black woman in Georgia to receive this honor.

Chapter Fourteen

Captain Molly

Pennsylvania, 1775

Margaret Corbin stirred the pot of stew, as her husband walked through the door. He glanced at her, removed his hat, and licked his lower lip. His expression told her what she needed. She walked to him with her hands on her hips and looked into his eyes.

"When do we leave?"

"I leave tomorrow," John said.

"*We* leave tomorrow. I'll start packing after we eat." The couple ate in relative silence, each deep in thought. They could no longer ignore the brewing trouble between the colonies and Britain. If they wanted freedom—and they did—they'd have to fight for it. But what would be their fate?

The next day, John, accompanied by Margaret, walked to the camp of the First Company of the Pennsylvania Artillery, commanded by Captain Thomas Proctor. John worked with the men while Margaret joined the other camp followers.

Immediately, she put her skills to use, nursing wounded soldiers. The army welcomed her help. Camp followers, women who accompanied the army, were allowed to stay if their work was considered vital to the army. If they did not contribute enough, or their work considered unnecessary, they were asked to leave. Margaret knew this and strived to be critical to the camp.

When not performing her tasks, Margaret spent little time with the other women. Their conversations of nursing and mending disinterested her. She preferred to watch her husband's unit perform their drills, including preparing and firing the cannon. It wasn't to merely pass the time. The precision and order fascinated her. She studied every move, every action. Her obsession with the artillery amused the soldiers.

One day she approached John and his crew. "Show me firsthand what to do," she demanded. John looked at the gunner who nodded to the others.

"After firing, we wipe down the cannon to extinguish any embers," one man explained, using a swab. "We swab it twice to be sure nothing remains. After that we're ready for another shot." He handed the swab to her so she could try. The men explained step-by-step what their responsibilities included.

Margaret, hungry to learn every detail, asked questions until she understood the routine. She learned the steps, taking a turn at each position. The men affectionately named her Captain Molly and admired her determination to train on the artillery.

In 1776, John's company was ordered to Fort Washington, New York. Margaret and other camp followers marched with the men. According to intelligence, British and Hessian troops were marching to the fort, planning an attack. If this proved true, there would be no more simple drills.

Margaret walked in silence but her mind wandered. Was the intelligence accurate? What would they find at the fort? Would John and the other men survive? No matter what, she knew her skills would be needed...those of a camp follower or those of someone familiar with artillery. She vowed to help where needed. It didn't take long for her skills to be called into play.

The men were drilling as usual on November 15, when

a British officer rode toward the fort under a flag of truce. Colonel Robert Magaw of Pennsylvania, commander of Fort Washington, met the approaching officer.

"You're outnumbered. You have no chance. Surrender, or there will be no mercy," the British officer boasted loudly.

Magaw didn't hesitate with his response. "We will *not* surrender! And you will see how Patriots fight."

The British officer retreated to his forces, behind him raucous shouting from the fort in support to Magaw's response.

Margaret watched as Magaw prepared his men for battle. He ordered John's crew to set up two cannon on a ridge known as Fort Tryon, the first line of defense to the north of Fort Washington. Other defenses were set up to the east and the south. Cliffs along the Hudson River prevented the enemy from attacking from the west.

Helping her husband and his crew maneuver the cannon and artillery, Margaret worked through the afternoon. She carried gunpowder, arranged cannon balls, and brought buckets of water. Everything needed to be in place. Lives depended on it. This was no longer a drill, a practice. This was war.

On November 16, Hessian soldiers attacked Fort

Tryon under the leadership of Lt. General Wilhelm Baron von Knyphausen. Expecting an easy victory, the German commander sent in his first wave of soldiers. A vigorous volley of cannon fire from the Patriots thwarted the attack. The enemy retreated. Another wave of attack, another, and another followed. The Americans fought with all their might.

Margaret answered call after call of "Captain Molly, over here!" She tended the wounded, refilled water buckets, and reloaded muskets. Her muscles screamed in pain as she continued. Suddenly enemy fire hit one of John's crew. Margaret stepped in and began helping load the cannon.

Hour after hour the battle raged. Smoke from musket and cannon fire filled the air. The enemy advanced closer and closer, their musket fire hitting their targets. Bodies lay strewn over the battlefield as the fighting continued. Margaret reached to get a cannonball to hand to John, when he collapsed. A Hessian musket ball had hit its mark, killing him.

"John!" Margaret screamed. "No, please, John!" No response.

John, dead. Margaret shook her head. *John, dead. His dream of freedom…*

"His dream of freedom will *not* die," she vowed as she took over his role at the cannon. The battle raged for hours, but the enemy advanced. With help from others, she aimed the cannon at the Hessians, hitting her target. Her grief seemed to spur her on. Again and again, her aim was accurate. The enemy fell.

Her sure fire aim earned the attention of the enemy, and she found herself under attack. Musket balls and grapeshot hit around her, kicking up dirt all around. Then the assault hit its mark.

"I'm hit," she screamed, toward the crew. "Take over." Grapeshot and musket balls had hit her, mangling her left arm, rendering it useless. More shots struck her again, hitting her jaw and her breast. Her tenure at the cannon was over.

The Hessians marched forward overtaking Fort Tryon and the other defenses. Wounded and dead Americans peppered the battlefield. Margaret awaited the bayonet that she was sure would end her life. The British officer's warning, "there will be no mercy" repeated through her head as she saw the enemy approach. Instead, the advancing soldiers stepped over bodies and past the wounded.

The British and Hessians forced their way into Fort Washington, and despite his resolve to fight, Magaw recognized the inevitable and surrendered. The Americans were defeated. The wounded Patriots, including Margaret since she had been a combatant, were paroled and ferried across the Hudson River to Fort Lee, New Jersey.

Despite receiving medical attention, Margaret never fully recovered from her wounds. She lost the use of her left arm for the rest of her life. Those who served with her attested to her bravery and her contribution to fighting the enemy. As a result, since she was a disabled soldier, she received a pension authorized by the Continental Congress. She was the first woman to receive this pension.

Uncomfortable socializing with other women, Margaret preferred to spend time with soldiers who fought in the war, recounting their battles. They spoke of the fighting, the heat, the lost lives, and the pride of fighting for a new nation. She felt a sense of camaraderie with others who shared her experiences. She died before reaching her 50th birthday.

* * * * *

In 1926, the Daughters of the American Revolution located what they believed was Margaret's unmarked grave and had her reinterred with full military honors at the West Point Cemetery. Recent findings proved that the remains were not hers but those of an unknown male. The DAR held a rededication ceremony for this heroic American on May 1, 2018 on the grounds of West Point.

In addition, Fort Tryon Park in Manhattan, New York honors her with a plaque describing her bravery.

Glossary of Terms

Allegiance – Loyalty shown to a person, country, belief, etc.

Bloody Scouts – A group of Tory outlaws led by "Bloody Bill" Cunningham. They were given this name because of their cruelty to those who aided the Patriots.

British Parliament – A group of British people who made laws for Britain and the colonies.

Cannoneer – A member of the artillery who positions and fires the cannon.

Continental Army – Formed after the start of the Revolutionary War. Congress named General George Washington the commander-in-chief of this army.

Courier – A person who carries messages, packages, information, etc. to another.

Cowboys – Outlaws on the side of the British.

D.A.R. – Daughters of the American Revolution. An organization of women who can trace their roots to Patriots of the American Revolution. The organization emphasizes historical preservation, education, and patriotism.

Forage – Feed or fodder for horses or cattle; grass; hay.

Genteel – Polite, well mannered, or proper. "Genteel" women would not engage in anything that may produce conflict.

Guerilla warfare – A form of harassment or sabotage often involving quick strikes against the enemy.

Gunner – A member of the crew manning a cannon.

Hessians – German soldiers who fought on the side of the British during the American Revolution. The British paid the Hessians to fight for them.

Loyalists or Tories – American colonists loyal to King George and England who wanted to remain under British rule.

Militia – A body of armed civilians. During the American Revolution, the militia often gathered quickly to help the Continental Army.

Muster – To gather troops. At a moment's notice, the militia would be requested to gather or muster for action.

Patriots, Rebels, or Whigs – American colonists who rebelled against British rule and wanted independence.

Quakers – A religious group that believes in God, believes in peace, and does not take sides in times of war.

Quartering Act – Law enacted by the British Parliament requiring American colonists to house, give accommodations to, and feed British troops and horses. At times only rooms in the house were used, at other times the entire house was used forcing some colonists out of their homes.

Rebels, Whigs or Patriots – American colonists who rebelled against British rule and wanted independence.

Retreat – A withdrawal of military forces. To go back.

Revolutionary War – Sometimes called the American War for Independence. War between America and Britain.

Saboteur – A person who disrupts or obstructs the efforts of another.

Skinners – Outlaws who didn't favor either the British or Patriots.

Skirmish – A brief and somewhat small conflict during a war; not a full-scale battle.

Smuggle – To move goods illegally into or out of a country.

Stamp Act – Law enacted by the British Parliament requiring American colonists to pay a tax on newspapers and legal documents.

Strategy – A plan of military operations and/or movements in war.

Sugar Act – Law enacted by British Parliament requiring a tax on many goods coming into America. This curtailed much of the smuggling of molasses. As a result, it hurt trade with non-British countries and colonies and negatively affected the economy of America.

Tactical – Planned or deliberate, often related to obtaining a specific military end.

Tories or Loyalists – American colonists loyal to King George and Britain who wanted to remain under British rule.

Treason – A crime of betrayal against one's country, often punishable by death.

Whigs, Patriots or Rebels – American colonists who rebelled against British rule and wanted independence.

ABOUT THE AUTHOR

K.M. Waldvogel holds a Bachelor of Science degree in elementary education and a Master of Science degree in education. She taught fifth grade for four years and eighth grade language arts for ten years.

Teaching fifth grade social studies renewed her passion for American history and she began reading as many books as possible on the subject. While doing so, she wondered about the role of women in our country's fight for independence. Having always enjoyed writing, she decided to merge these two interests and began researching little-known women of the American Revolution. Her reading uncovered many heroic tales by young girls and women. The result of her research is *Spies, Soldiers, Couriers, and Saboteurs: Women of the American Revolution*.

Waldvogel is also the author of a Halloween picture book, *Three Little Ghosts*. She is a member of the Society of Children Book Writers and Illustrators, Wisconsin Writers Association, and local writing groups in Wisconsin and Arizona. She and her husband reside in Wisconsin but spend many happy months each year in Arizona.

You can follow her on Facebook at *https://www.facebook.com/author.KM.Waldvogel.*